

Made in the USA
Coppell, TX
08 May 2025

49111696R00069